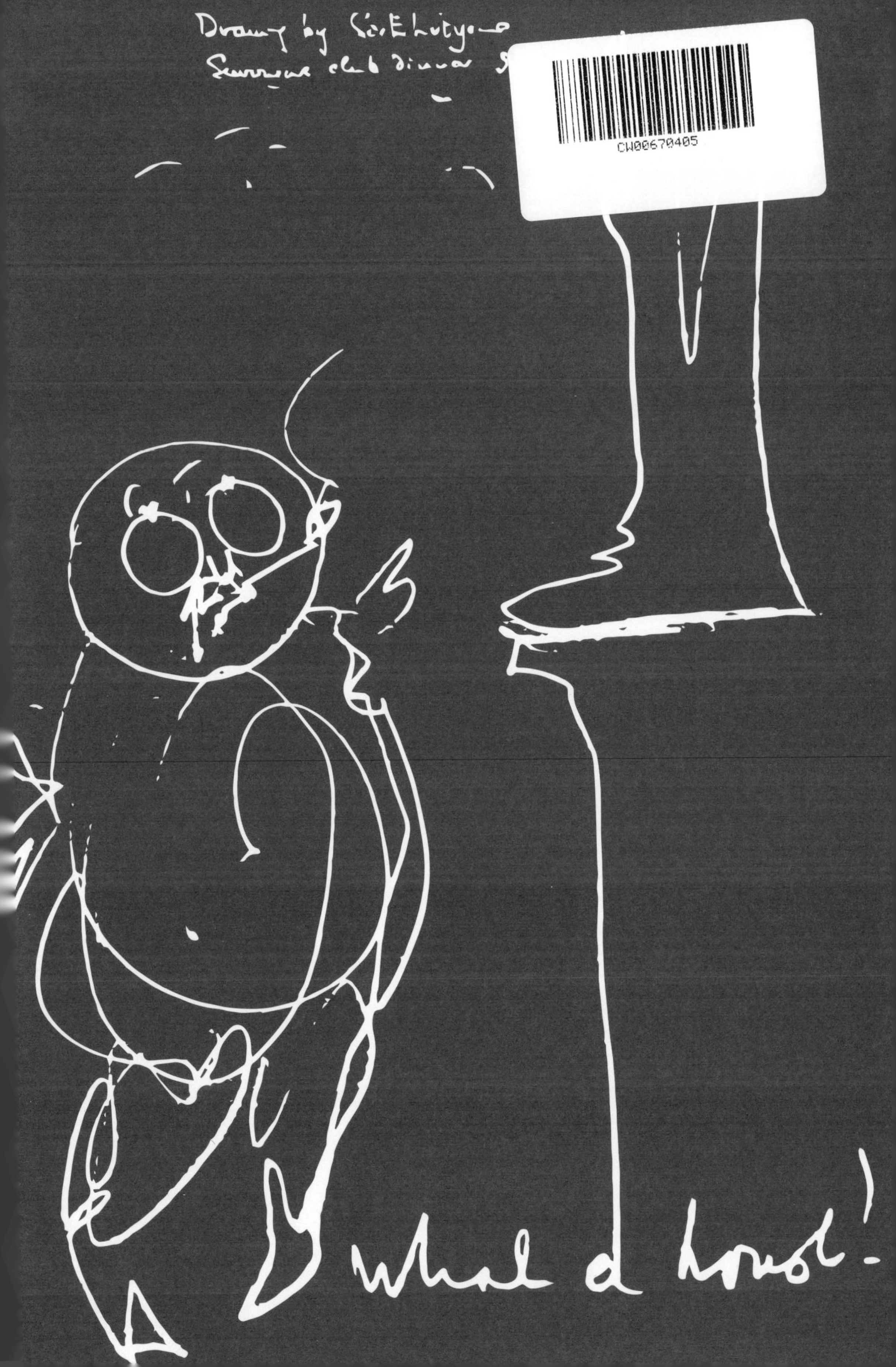
Drawing by Sir E Lutyens
Surveyors club dinner
What a knob!

"LUT"

Mark Twain (signature)

"LUT"

Life in the Office of Sir Edwin Lutyens

Edited by Mark Lutyens

Anthony Eyre

MOUNT ORLEANS PRESS

To my father, Charles Lutyens
1928-2017

Published in Great Britain in 2022
by Anthony Eyre, Mount Orleans Press
23 High Street, Cricklade SN6 6AP
www.anthonyeyre.com

© Mark Lutyens 2022

Mark Lutyens has asserted his right to be
identified as the author of this work in accordance with
the Copyright, Designs and Patents Act 1988.

ISBN 978-1-912945-35-1

A CIP record for this book is available
from the British Library

Printed in the UK by
Short Run Press

Contents

PA1625

Foreword

THIS IS A real cracker... Who knew that the gifted and very young men working in the office of the great Sir Edwin Lutyens as apprentices, pupils and assistants, got up to such tricks?

A hitherto unknown bunch of letters and comical sketches, found by a family member in a trunk, recall anecdotes and memories sufficient to make a modern Health and Safety officer's hair stand on end. One game involved lying down on the drawing-table, worming your way round to the underside, and inching along upside-down before reappearing at the other end, and wriggling your way back to the top. Then there were the stool-hopping races. It must have been really noisy. However did they get the work done, during these years of Lutyens' most monumental productivity? One of their more fantastical bright ideas, when Lutyens was redesigning the interior of the Grange at Rottingdean, was to run a glass soil-pipe across the drawing-room floor—a memory particularly treasured by the informant. Maybe routing the plumbing was proving a bit of a challenge?

Elegantly designed, informatively edited and annotated, this little book is not only a wholly unexpected insight into Lutyens' world, and a curiosity, but in itself a treasure.

Victoria Glendinning

Introduction

GIVEN THE number of books, articles and anecdotes about the life and works of Sir Edwin Lutyens, one might suppose there was little left to discover. It was therefore a surprise and delight to receive from my cousin, Mark Lutyens, a packet of letters from architects who had worked as pupils or assistants in Sir Edwin's office, where they knew him as ELL.

The letters were previously unknown and reading them made it clear that they were prompted by Mark's grandfather Eadred, a nephew of ELL, who had worked for a time in his uncle's office. Eadred had written to other alumni of the office, asking for their recollections of amusing incidents and anecdotes from their life there.

The replies which Eadred received form the core of this book and I am very grateful to Mark for commissioning it and writing the supporting text. The letters paint a picture of a congenial office life, embracing the pranks and jokes that one would expect of an organisation with ELL at its centre. Nonetheless, these young men clearly held ELL in awe and there are references to the occasional explosion from his office, when work failed to meet his exacting standards; and there is no mistaking the meticulous thoroughness and accuracy which were demanded of all who worked there.

It is hard to resist quoting from the letters in this introduction; but that would dilute the fun of them and the affection which the writers clearly felt for ELL and so defeat the point of the book.

There is, though, a sombre footnote to these light-hearted and sometimes hilarious letters. In December 1938, ELL returned from his final visit to India. While there he had suffered acute pneumonia, from which he is thought never to have fully recovered: a sad conclusion to his immense achievements there. His spirits must, however, have been lifted when, a few days after his return, he was elected President of the Royal Academy: only the third architect to hold that office. As his daughter Mary relates "The honour, he said, was as great a surprise to him, as if he had been elected Pope".

The excitement of this appointment must, however, have been tempered by the outbreak, a few months later of WW2, scarcely twenty years from the ending of the Great War, in which several of the letter-writers had served and in which ELL's family had lost five sons, including two of Eadred's brothers.

The war and further illness put an effective stop to ELL's practice, though he remained busy working on his plans for Liverpool Roman Catholic Cathedral and on the Bressey-Lutyens Plan for the post-war future of Greater London. And in the New Year Honours List of 1942 he became the first architect to receive the Order of Merit—another tribute to his extraordinary life and achievements.

In the concluding years until his death on New Year's Day 1944, I do wonder whether Eadred went to see him. If he did, I hope he took with him the letters reproduced in this book and that the two architects were able to laugh together at the happy memories they record.

Martin Lutyens
Chairman of the Lutyens Trust 2001-2021

"It was all a grand experience"

IN 1939, my grandfather, Eadred Lutyens, wrote to a number of former colleagues and fellow architects asking them to send him their memories of the years they had spent as assistants to his uncle, Sir Edwin Lutyens O.M. Clearly, he had some sort of publication in mind—there are references to it in the letters he received in reply—but it never happened; war came, times changed and, strange as it may now seem, Sir Edwin's reputation languished and the moment passed.

Four years ago, 2018, in an old trunk, I found some letters—together with a number of sketches, old magazines and news clippings, souvenirs and nameless photographs; general memorabilia which my father Charles had dutifully stored but never sorted. I have to admit that I didn't at first recognise the value of them. It is thanks to my cousin Martin Lutyens that I didn't burn them, he pointed out that they were both amusing and of potential interest to a wider audience, and suggested that we should consider publishing them, fulfilling Eadred's original intention and the expectations of those who had sent them. They provide a vivid, first-hand account of life in the office of Sir Edwin Lutyens as told by those who worked there.

This book reproduces all 21 pages, 11 letters in effect, all written by architects some of whom went on to become household names. Where I can, I will provide a brief biography of those men (they are all men) who I can trace, and say a little about the context in which they were written. This is by no means a definitive study—indeed my research has been limited by the Covid crisis and the fact that the RIBA library, where much of the surviving material from Lutyens' office is now stored, is temporarily closed—my intention is simply to convey a sense of what it must have been like to work in what was the most fashionable architectural practice of its day, and also to pay tribute to Eadred Lutyens who did the initial spadework. There isn't an actual letter from Eadred but elsewhere, I have found some reminiscences which I have included.

We don't quite know what Eadred's proposal was but it is very likely that this project was prompted by a dinner at the Café Royal earlier in that year, on 24th February 1939, which was attended by many of the men who had worked in Sir Edwin's office over the previous 40 years or so—pupils, assistants and improvers (*'a C19 architectural assistant, working wholly or partly gratis in order to enhance knowledge or skills'*—'work experience' perhaps). The dinner was to celebrate Sir Edwin's appointment as PRA (President of the Royal Academy) but perhaps also his forthcoming 70th birthday—he was born on 29th March 1869. I picture this happy group, white ties and medals, sprawling over the port, conscious of the history of the moment and discussing the need to preserve for posterity their combined experience of life in the great man's office before all was forgotten and lost. It was percipient, in a few months time another war would begin, Sir Edwin would be dead, the practice would close and many of the drawings and other records dispersed if not thrown away; a new dark age.

Eadred Lutyens (1891-1974) was the fourth child of Charles Benjamin Lutyens (1853-1922), Edwin's eldest brother, the oldest of

Eadred Lutyens

fourteen children. Their father, Charles Henry Augustus Lutyens (1820-1916) was a vigorous figure; tall and athletic, a sportsman, as were many of his children—the youngest, the Reverend William ('Canon Bill' because he was so fast) held the world record for the 1000 yard sprint for twenty years—Ned was the exception, his only interest in country sports was fishing. Like his father, General Charles Lutyens, C.H.A. Lutyens joined the army and was posted to Montreal where he met and married the Governor's sister, Mary Gallwey (later described by Emily Lytton, Ned's fiance, as *'beautiful, vague and serene'*). He served in the Crimean War where, because he could draw, he acted as a reconnaisance officer ranging ahead of the advancing army, recording in rapid sketches the detail of the topography of the country into which they were marching. He was however, more than a dilettante artist, he was an inventor and an able mathematician too. Whilst

13

Aug. 7. 1902.

Dear Barby.

We are sending you two little
happy returns of the day. We hope
at Felixstowe. We are all
fat, as there is now so
no to eat at tea — because
have gone away these look like this:

uncle Hoddart. —

Have you seen the Snail?

uncle Milne. — Un

Please give

FROM MR. E. L. LUTYENS,

29, BLOOMSBURY SQUARE,

LONDON, W.C.

This is a picture of my friend the snail.

...icture books to wish you many ...u are having a very good time ...tting very ...uch cake for you + Robert

...ppo   Uncle Evans.   Uncle Thomas.   Uncle Aylwin.

love to Robert   Your affectionate uncles. in the office of 29. Bloomsbury Square.

C.H.A. Lutyens painting a horse

in the army, he designed and patented an artillery range-finder
which was still in use at the beginning of wwi; and, as an Inspector
of Musketry, recommended that the British army adopt and
develop the American breech-loading rifle—they didn't but the
Germans did with devastating consequences. In 1857 he resigned
his commission to become a professional painter and sculptor of
animals; primarily horses, hounds and hunting scenes. He had
considerable success, employed by many of the leading patrons of
his day, including the royal family, managing to raise and educate
a very large family; to have a house in what was then fashionable
and artistic West London (16 Onslow Sq); and a house in Surrey
(The Cottage, Thursley). He shared a studio with the sculptor,
Marochetti, helping him to model the lions in Trafalgar Square,

and was a close friend of Sir Edwin Landseer who, being childless, one day asked if he could have one of Lutyens' many children— "You have so many, I only want one"—Charles declined but offered instead to make him the godfather of his next child whom he christened Edwin Landseer Lutyens—Ned!

From his father, Ned inherited not only artistic genius, stamina and determination but also his intuitive understanding of the way things work, how they fit together. It was said of Charles' paintings and sculptures of animals "not the least part of his art was that every muscle was seen under the skin"—like father, like son, they both had an exceptional eye for detail. From his Irish mother, he inherited the warmer aspects of his character which so endeared him to his clients and those who worked with him—he seemed to generate a real affection in a profession which can be somewhat overly-serious and cold-hearted. ELL joked that whilst he regarded his staff as his children, he couldn't say as much because it would involve too many explanations to his wife!

When I try to visualise Sir Edwin I think of my grandfather, Eadred—funny, silly ("have I told you the story of the three wells? well, well, well…") and always busy, either doing something or, as I remember it, trying to get us to amuse him. He was easily bored and prone to fits of exasperation—fishing with him once, he flung his favourite rod in the river, turned and strode away. Eadred was born in 1891. His father's tea plantation in Ceylon had finally 'come good' but not before he had nearly bankrupted his father which impacted heavily on the younger members of the family who were still at home, reducing them to an eccentric poverty—newspaper instead of a table cloth and the whole family feeding from a single plate—memories of which apparently haunted Ned his whole life.

Eadred was one of the pages at Ned's wedding to Emily Lytton in

August 1897—a copy of the wedding invitation hangs on the wall at Goddards. *"Later, when at the Architectural College, I used to take my drawings over for him to see. Instead of my playing rugby football on Saturday afternoon, he used to urge me to go down to St. Pauls, study some part and go home and draw it out. I am sorry to say that 'football' always had the day".*

His studies were interrupted by the war. He joined up in 1914 and fought first in Palestine and then on the Western Front. He survived, unlike his two older brothers, Charles (again) and Graeme who were killed. Their deaths, together with that of his father soon after, left a hole in his life which I think Edwin may well have helped fill. He was clearly fond of his uncle whom he admired hugely, and that affection was returned—printed here is a charming letter from Ned to Eadred congratulating him on his engagement. It is perhaps not surprising therefore, that of all the many assistants who could have done it, it was Eadred who elected, or was chosen, to gather and compile a record of life in the office of ELL (as they refer to him in the letters).

Despite the allure of sport, Eadred did eventually become an architect in his late twenties—a good one too although somewhat eclipsed by his uncle. In 1943 he became a fellow of the RIBA, Edwin acting as one of his sponsors. When Eadred went to see Uncle Ned to ask if he would sign the form, Ned, without hesitation, signed it. Eadred, not a little surprised, said "But you haven't seen any of my recent work". "Oh but I have" replied Ned "I have seen your two boys".

The following is from Eadred's memoir: *"In 1920 he took me into his office in Queen Anne's Gate at first where most of the war memorials were being drawn out. Later I went when most of the office was moved to work on Delhi in Apple Tree Yard off Jermyn Street. I was there for two years and worked on one wing, the S.W. wing for the entire time. There*

13, MANSFIELD STREET,

W.1.

July. 14. 27.

My dear Sackville

I am so glad —

Bless you. both of you

Do bring her — & show HER off!

Ermine will be back at the end of
this — the beginning of next
month.

Ever affectionately
Uncle Ned

was not a single drawing sent out from the office that he did not see and correct if necessary. It was incredible how he could draw free hand to any scale, and when he checked with a scale it would be correct. Everyone was very much on their toes, as any shoddy work was immediately torn up, quite regardless of the amount of work put in. One assistant had been busy drawing out the India Memorial Arch for several weeks, and finally went in to Sir Edwin's room with a bundle of drawings to every scale, under his arm. There was a few moments silence and then an explosion with a rending tearing sound, and out came his assistant, purple in the face, and holding a tattered remnant of his bundle. Nothing further was done on the memorial for several weeks to come. Another assistant had been a bit slack on a detail concerned with something on a flat roof. He stupidly said "No one will see it" — "Yes, God will" came the immediate reply. In 1922 I left for 3 months to do a tour of Italy with two friends. When in Florence a message came to the hotel at which we were staying to say that Mr "J", an American architect, would be pleased if we would join him in a visit to Lucca to see the villas there on the next day. Naturally we accepted. It all went well and we made good friends. Later he came to England and, together with Mr. Austin Hall, we made him out a list of important places and houses to see. He was away several months and one day, when I was back in the office, I was told he wanted to see me. Whereupon he asked if Sir Edwin was in. He was in and I asked him if he would see the American architect. In he rushed and started with a terrific flow of words; "You will be glad to know, Mr. Lutyens, that in our country your book is our bible. Hardly a house goes up which has not got your doors, your windows, your chimneys or your roofs." There was a pause, and then Sir Edwin said rapidly and quietly: "Why don't you think it out yourself?" I have never seen anyone so crushed as Mr. "J", but he soon recovered and they were last seen with Sir Edwin's arm round his shoulder leading him to the door" (Eadred Lutyens).

It is well known that Edwin Lutyens had little or no formal education and very limited experience of life in a conventional practice before setting up on his own at the astonishingly young age of 20. It is not surprising therefore, that his office as it grew was somewhat idiosyncratic. It was like a beehive, ELL being the central focus, everything arranged to service his prodigious output. At its peak there were as many as 17 people in the office and yet he remained somewhat apart from the hurly-burly, forever a shy man and keen to avoid confrontation. Young men came and went and some, as they do now, had their own small commissions on the side. One such was accused of plagiarising one of ELL's designs and was sent to see him to explain and apologise. This was the sort of conversation that Sir Edwin dreaded. As the young man began to speak, Edwin, flustered, and possibly slightly irritated at being interupted, cut him off saying "No, I didn't believe it was true either. You simply wouldn't do such a thing" patted him on back and sent him back to his drawing board.

He was always a little uneasy at having to work with such a large number of high-spirited young men—a reminder perhaps of his own chaotic childhood—and he coped with it by always managing to have a room to himself which was, by all accounts, an invariably bleak and brutally bare space, a place to think, work and avoid the general distractions of the busy office next door—and puff away on his pipe which his wife, Emily, suggested was a smoke screen; literally, a defense against the world. Having said that, some of his young men's more bizzare antics, such as crawling across the top of a table and back under its underside without touching the floor, would have amused him—he was after all, only a few years older than many of them and, in the early days, his was the youngest and most exciting practice in town. But, why did so many come and go? It might have been the pressure but it might also have been because that was what he expected them to do—as he had done himself. Herbert Baker, recalling the short time they had together in the office of Sir Ernest George as paying apprentices (then THE practice in which to get a placement; also known as the Eton of Architects) "*I first met Lutyens there, who, though joking through his short pupillage, quickly absorbed all that was best worth learning: he puzzled us at first, but we soon found that he seemed to know by intuition some great truths about our art which was not to be learnt there*".

Being largely self-taught and having learnt most of what he knew from observation and first principles, it must have baffled him that such self-evident truths were not obvious to all. '*Why don't you think it out for yourself?*'—it must have been said, or thought, a thousand times. Having apparently never really struggled to find a solution to any architectural problem, he would have found it difficult to understand that others might, that they were unable to appreciate the beauty and inevitable logic of a good, elegant design. In one of Margaret Richardson's many essays which she wrote for the catalogue of the Arts Council exhibition at the Hayward Gallery in the winter of 1981, she says "*Lutyens took into consideration the quantitive relationships of every part of the plan, and the meticulous and interdependent proportions which ensued involved the most extraordinary fractions... He would admit of no approximation in the drawings, on the plea that plenty of inaccuracies would creep in without beginning in the office. 'About! I don't know what you mean by 'about'', he would say*". He was exacting, and he drove himself and those around him hard but even if he was not an easy man to work for, the education and sheer fun of it clearly outweighed the drudge—as Paul Phipps (1901-1903) wrote "*It was all a grand experience*". And, they didn't do it for the money either: like Sir Ernest George, he did not pay a good wage but always gave them a very good reference.

Lutyens left Sir Ernest George's office after only a year, in 1889, when he landed his first large commission, Crooksbury in Surrey. One thing he did take with him was Sir Ernest's beguiling presentation technique using soft pen and wash sketches viewed from ground level, the 'worm's eye view', which was to become ELL's hallmark too. He worked first from his father's house in London, 16 Onslow Square, where he stayed until late 1893, working alone, night and day, producing a huge volume of work including designs for his first large house, Chinthurst Hill near Guildford. He then moved to his first office at 6 Gray's Inn Square where he took on an assistant, William Barlow—*"Old Barlow, Lutyens' first assistant, a tragic figure with a tragic history... bearded and silent under a window, usually working out calculations with a slide rule."* (Paul Phipps, ca 1902). They must have made an odd couple, the young, effervescent Edwin and the elderly, serious and deeply religious ex-clerk of works.

By 1898 there were seven assistants, a secretarial assistant, Dalton, and an officer manager, E. Baynes Badcock, who was the closest ELL ever came to having a business partner. They were good friends however, the arrangement seems to have been informal and, in 1902, ended with considerable ill-feeling (providing plenty of opportunity for some bad puns)—and to cap it all Mr Dalton did a bunk with the office cash. Despite these teething problems, things then improved. A.J. Thomas came to manage the office and stayed until 1935. He was joined by E.E. Hall as his assistant and between them the office started to run like a well-oiled machine, stable and highly productive. And at the heart of the office were the long stayers, the real motive force. They were:

Sid Evans (1900-1925), George Stewart (1911-1944), Trevor Owen (1925-1935) and Arthur Shoosmith (1920-1931). They guaranteed a consistently high level of output, both quality and quantity, servicing an increasingly busy office, with projects all over the world. And behind the scenes, Beatrice Webb the office secretary—

> "W's Miss Webb, our guardian and sister, and
> X the excitement there'd be if we missed her"
> *(The Office Alphabet by A.H. Gardner—one of the letters reproduced here).*

and Mr Tribe, a former bus driver, who acted as a general factotum, not the least of his duties to fill six pipes every morning for Sir Edwin to smoke throughout the day.

It is extraordinary just how much work the office did manage to produce given the limitations of technology and communication then as compared to now—telephones, travel, computers for both design and information storage, printing techniques and the ability to transmit information fast and over unlimited distances. And yet, arguably, the output was of a higher intrinsic quality than anything we make today with all our modern advantages. Christopher Hussey, shortly after Ned's death, with access still to those who knew him, writing by far and away the best book about his life and work, said *"The quantity, however, though exceeding that of any other noted English architect, including Wren, is less significant than the quality and variety of his work. No detail of this was ever delegated to an assistant... No drawing left the office without his personal approval of it, or before, (in most cases) it had been repeatedly revised"* Or, A.H. Gardner, again, puts it more succinctly *"...D are the drawings we've so often cursed..."*

Whilst the construction drawings that left the office were famously thorough, there were a few 'golden rules' that evolved over the years which further eliminated uncertainty—simplicity being one (almost certainly a reaction against Victorian fussiness and clutter)—others concerned proportion and stock mathematical ratios, often quite sophisticated, such as the angle of a roof must always be at 54.45 degrees to produce an intersection of the two planes at, magically, 45 degrees. Sacred geometry perhaps but it is this inevitable simplicity and honest approach to architecture which so endears Ned and his work to all regardless of style and creed—he never fudged it—as he said, someone (God) will see and appreciate the effort.

Sir Edwin lived in London—the promise he made to his wife when they married that he would build her a little white house in the country never materialised—and this is where his offices were as well, often all under one roof e.g. 29 Bloomsbury Square and 13 Mansfield Street. In reality, the creative heart of the practice was always ELL, as he moved from place to place, there was its centre. And then, as now, every project would also have had its own site office where the contractor kept the working drawings and other paperwork and where the architect, when on site, would have worked them up; details sketched in the margins, on scraps of paper, and, as with Sir Edwin, his 'virgins', the small, pocket-sized sheets of paper he used to illustrate and record his ideas. He carried them with him wherever he went—a coarse paper cut to A5 size, a hole punched in one corner, held together with a piece of string. On the top sheet he would sketch an idea, tear it off and give it to whoever he was talking to—whether client, assistant or contractor. These are the sketches my grandfather collected and which I found with the letters—one of them is reproduced below. On the larger projects a temporary or satellite office was set up—at Castle Drogo for instance, a room in the hotel in Exeter in which the team stayed, was used, and for New Delhi they used a cabin onboard ship for the long journey out and back.

The following is a list of ELL's main offices: 6 Gray's Inn Square, until 1897 when he married; then 29 Bloomsbury Square—the office on the ground floor; the family living above; 17 Queen Anne's Gate (1919-1930); 7 Apple Tree Yard—'the Delhi Office' (it amused him that he was designing a palace in a coachman's cottage); and finally 13 Mansfield Street which had been his home since 1919 and had been used occasionally (e.g. the Queen's dolls' house and Liverpool Cathedral) and then more permanently from about 1931 when the lease on 17 Queen Anne's Gate expired.

I will leave the last word to Paul Phipps: "Even if these few lines are of no use to you, it has been great fun remembering… the good times and good fellows connected with it".

The Letters

Evelyn Waugh.

Stone edging cool light grey.

Distant tree cool dk foliage
lawn tree pa plum.
Cream stone
Distant Roof purplish red tile

E. H. BEALE, A.R.I.B.A.,
REGISTERED AND CHARTERED
ARCHITECT.

TEL. BURWASH 81.

ROCKHURST,
BURWASH.
SUSSEX.

7. 4. 39.

Dear Mr Lutyens.

I think it an excellent idea to collect "Lut" stories in some permanent form, and I hope we shall all be able to aquire a copy of whatever you may produce.

The only personal thing I remember was when I took a staircase drawing to ask what was wanted. The stairs went up three sides of the well and the fourth side had a landing. Lutyens wanted the underside of the landing domed in its length and in its width. Both curves to be continued down on the soffit of the string of the stairs. He explained all this in his usual quick and inaudible way and ended by saying "you see, just cut it out of an orange". I did not see but was

Left: Campion Hall Garden with the distant figure of Evelyn Waugh, sketch by Charles Mahoney.

too alarmed to say so, being told "to take it away" and had to go and get help in the office.

A short while ago I met an artist at some friends here who had done some painting in Campion Hall Oxford for Lutyens. And he told me of his difficulties when trying to get sizes etc from Lut. How Lut mumbled and walked away from him round the table he following. ~~But~~ And when it came to the done, he too was ~~told to~~ "cut it out of an orange."

There was an elderly lady living here who in her youth remembered how shocked the Victorians were at a dance, when Lutyens's partner asked him if he did not think a certain girl very pretty and Lut said he did not, he was thinking what she would look like with no clothes on. But most of the best stories one only knows secondhand. But I hope to find them all incorporated in your book. Yours sincerely

J. H. Beale.

BERTRAM CARTER, A.R.I.B.A., 28 THEOBALD'S ROAD, GRAY'S INN, LONDON, W.C.I

REGISTERED CHARTERED ARCHITECT   TELEPHONE: CHANCERY 7980 - ELTHAM 1673

April,
Twenty One,
1 9 3 9 .

Eadred Lutyens, Esq., A.R.I.B.A.,
1 Port Hill,
Hertford.

My dear Lutyens,

        I am quite ashamed of myself for my neglect to
your two letters and particularly for missing the dinner to
Sir Edwin which I was very sorry not to have attended.

        The one or two anecdotes which I treasure I
doubt if they are quite suitable although charming in themselves.
One in particular concerned a glass soil pipe passing through
the drawing room at the Grange, Rottingdean, and I would like
to tell you it. I expect you remember the American Architect
who visited us and who had an introduction to Sir Edwin. When
this visitor related to him that "We use your windows, your
doors, your dormers, your chimney stacks in America", Sir Edwin
replied: "You go back and tell them to think for themselves".
Another one which possibly Thomas has told you was a little
trouble over the datum pane. Apparently some dormers looked
into a valley and it was structurally difficult to work in the
pane. Thomas after a long argument complained that in any case
no one could see it to which Sir Edwin snapped up: "yes they can".
"Well who can"? "Why, God can of course". But these are not so
nice as my soil pipe which I simply must tell you.

        Kindest regards,

                Yours sincerely,

                Bertram Carter.

C. M. C. Armstrong, F.R.I.B.A.
A. H. Gardner, A.R.I.B.A.

Telephone 4755

19 Eaton Road,
Coventry
and at 39 High St.,
Warwick

25.3.39.

Dear Mr. Lutyens,

Thank you for your note. I should
hesitate to repeat the traditional office
stories as it is difficult to separate
truth from legend, though I should hate to
think that they belong to anything but the
first category.

The enclosed office alphabet which I
was rash enough to compose may however be
of some interest. If you feel a glossary
is necessary, no doubt you will let me know.

I have just been reminded of a ritual
in the top office of Queen Anne's Gate.
This consisted of lying on the central table
(cleared for the purpose) and climbing underneath and up the other side without touching
the floor. I think most of us passed this
test at one time or another. I also
remember a hopping race on office stools
(which I believe I won). This nearly brought
the office down, in a literal manner.

Yours faithfully,

A. H. Gardner.

E.J.T. Lutyens Esq., A.R.I.B.A.,
1, Port Hill,
Hertford.

AN OFFICE ALPHABET
for Sir Edwin Lutyens Office.

A stands for A.J.T. thankless his lot is,
B's the word blank, overworked by the office.
C's C.T. Ayerst whom we couldn't get first,
D are the drawings we've so often cursed,
E is Sir Edwin, our Master and Lord,
F are the Flappers we wave to when bored,
G's Garrett, Gardner and Greenwood as well,
H stands for Hough, our Liverpudlian swell.
I is the ink from India far,
J is for James who calls round with the car,
K is young Kain-that cheery young cod,
L is the angle of fifty four odd.
M is Macdonald our Badminton fan,
N's number 17, Home of the Clan,
O is for Owen, who thinks he can sing,
P stands for Percy-the abdomen king.
Q's Queen Anne's Gate, frequented by kites
R-rubber necking to see all the sights,
S is for Stewart, our oldest survivor,
T's office Tea - a much needed reviver.
U is the unit that E.L.L. favours,
V's Vincent Brooks whom we keep by our labours.
W's Miss Webb, our guardian and sister, and
X the excitement there'd be if we missed her.
Y's the young Butes we occasionally see, while
Z's quite impossible, as you'll agree.

                              A.H. Gardner,
                              Jan.   1929.

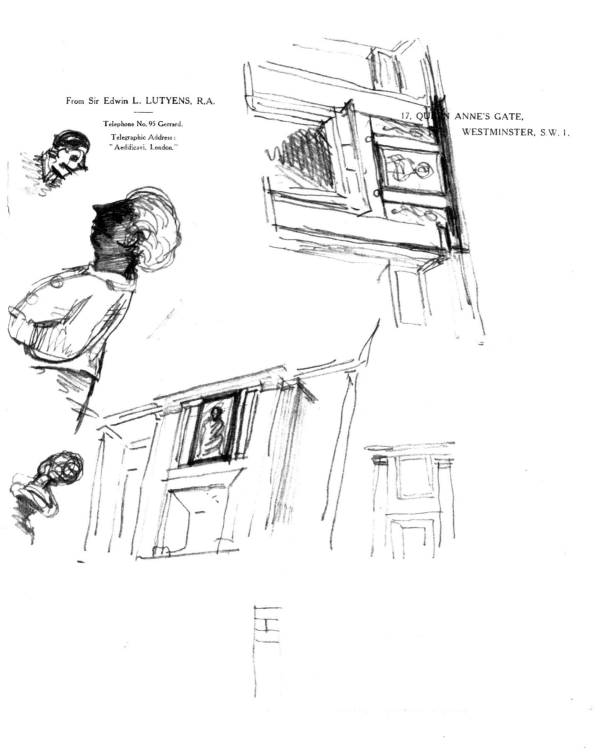

From Sir Edwin L. LUTYENS, R.A.

Telephone No. 95 Gerrard.

Telegraphic Address:
"Aedificavi, London."

17, QUEEN ANNE'S GATE,
WESTMINSTER, S.W. 1.

Doodles by Lutyens on office paper

28. 3. 39.

Dear Mr. Lutyens, Owing to the war & being
no doubt rather a dull dog anyhow, my memory
of incidents in Sir Edwin' Office is not too
good. I do however recollect that he made
in the kitchen of Lord Overstrand's house an
enormous circular window the raison d'être
of which was not quite obvious.

Sir Edwin explained that Lord Overstrand's
French chef being as nearly a sphere as any
human being could be, the window was designed
for him to escape by in case of fire. What-
could be more appropriate & fitting!

It was with great regret that
I saw someone else was made pope
instead of Sir Edwin as I had been

hoping for "another jolly dinner".

Yours sincerely

R. M. F. Huddart

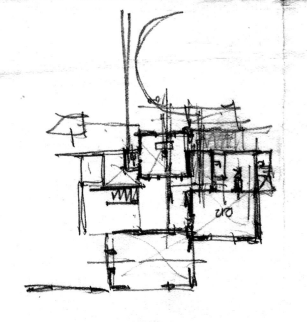

3 London Road,
High Wycombe.
Bucks.

March 28th. 1939.

Eadrid Lutyens, Esq.
1 Port Hill,
Hertford.

Dear Sir.
           In reply to your letter re. the collection
of anecdotes concerning Sir Edwin, I add a few below
which I hope may be of some use to you.
I am afraid that, compared with most of the tales
about Sir Edwin, these are very trivial, but I have
restricted my efforts to incidents in which I was
more or less involved or for which I can personally
vouch.
The first occurred after I had been with him for a
mere six months. By means of living on bread and water
for that period I had scraped together enough hard cash
to buy a copy of "Houses and Gardens".
One day, greatly daring, I took it down to him for him
to sign. He was very charming about it all and sat
down, pen in hand, mumbling vaguely "DearmewashalIput? (I am
afraid it is quite impossible to convey on this type-
-writer those quaint, sort of adenoidal, sounds that he
produces when he is talking of one thing and thinking
of something entirely different!) After a moment he wrote,
to my amazement and my surprise,--"In great regard", E.L.L.
I was just thinking what the devil of a fellow I must
be to receive such an inscription after a mere six
months when Sir Edwin turned round and said, "I have
put; In great regard", as I thought there might be a blank
cheque under the page! Still, when I shew the book to
my frrends they naturally think what I first thought
and I hate disillusioning them, so it works out alright
in the long run!
One afternoon a friend of mine was rushing downstairs
with an eaves detail for which the printer was waiting.
As he was passing Sir Edwin's room, Sir Edwin came
wandering out and demanded to know what he (Bailey) had got.
Bailey, in a great hurry just said "Eaves Sir,--full size
detail". "Oh" replied Sir Edwin, "Haven't you done a full
size of Adam's as well!"
Mr. Stewart will no doubt vouch for the next as he was
directly concerned. He had jst done some drawings for a
War Memorial in Rhodesia and the job had been estimated
at a simply prohibitive figure. As the drawing stood
there were no dimensions on it, merely the scale.
With great resource Sir Edwin remarked "OH, never mind,
Alter the scale from $\frac{1}{4}$" to $\frac{1}{2}$" and see what it comes
out at!" This actually gave a figure of less than a
quarter the original one and I believe that it was
submitted to the authorities in this form!
I am afraid that I cannot remember any more, that I have
any right to relate, but will let you ahve any that may
wecur to me within the next week or so.
If there is any publication resultant from these united
efforts I shall be most grateful to be allowed to suscribe,
within the normally restricted limits of a younger member
of this impecunious profession! With many thanks and
best wishes in your search.

                              Yours faithfull

Sid Evans.

1903

OSWALD P. MILNE. F.R.I.B.A.
ARCHITECT.
CHARTERED & REGISTERED
Welbeck 7105

64, WIGMORE STREET,
LONDON, W.1.

3rd May 1939.

Dear Eadrid,

I received your printed form asking for incidents
that happened when one was in Sir Edwin's Office.

I have nothing very definite to relate, but I have
put down a few notes of abiding impressions of that time.

Alas! you should have said over a period of 40 years
and not 30, that Sir Edwin had congenial relations with
his assistants and pupils.   It was in the very early
years of the century that I spent some two years in the
office in Bloomsbury Square.

We were then all youthful assistants of a young master
who was already earning fame with his imaginative and
charming country houses and his inventive use of materials.
His reputation was already becoming international as was
shown by the fact that Wallick, an American, and Bamford,
a New Zealander, on their arrival in England had insisted
on becoming his pupils.

Assistants and pupils all worked together in the large

room behind E.L.L.'s front room office.   Syd Evans,
who must be known to many who have passed through the office,
was already well established in the office traditions when
I arrived as an assistant.   He had his own peculiar dry
jokes and stories.   One of the most honoured of these was
of the waiter who walked so much in serving his clients
that he wore off his feet and then had to turn up the ends
of his legs so as to carry on.

Paul Phipps, just down from Oxford, had a ready pencil
as a caricaturist, and combining this with wit, banter and
leg pull, he would drive Wallick to fury, after which he
would insist on shaking hands with "hands across the sea,
Wallick, hands across the sea".

There were as pupils, Huddart, from a Yorkshire Rectory,
better known as the 'Infant Prodigy' and Beau Hannen, who
from the building tradition of his family, was destined by
them to be an Architect, but whose heart was more upon stage
matters than on half inch and full size details.   Presently
he abandoned the 'noble art' and became famous as Nicholas
Hannen, the actor.

In those days E.L.L. lived above the shop and there was
a certain domestic air about the offices on the ground floor.
The young family, consisting at that time of 'Barbie' and
Robert, were often, on returning from their afternoon walk,

brought into the office by their nurse, and were regaled with lumps of sugar. Tea was sure to be brewing, for Alwyn, who had joined the Staff, used to start boiling the kettle as soon as he returned from lunch.

Lutyens was himself a great worker, and very often descended to the office again after dinner and worked till midnight, and for weeks together, if there was a press of work, we would return to our drawing boards after a dinner interval and continue translating the sketches that flowed from our Master's pencil into working drawings.

Yours sincerely,

A. TREVOR OWEN, A.R.I.B.A.,
Chartered Architect.

Tel : PAD. 6841.

118, GEORGE STREET,
LONDON, W.1.

March 29th. 1939

Dear Mr Lutyens,

     In reply to your request for anecdotes relating to
Sir Edwin, I recall the following amusing stories if you think
them worth recording in your permanent collection.

I.   During a visit to a London House to which Sir Edwin was
making additions and alterations, a newsboy passed by with a
placard headline in large type, "Lord Byng dead". The Client
who happened to be a retired Army Colonel remarked to Sir Edwin,
"By jove, Byng's dead", and Sir Edwin's immediate reply was,
Oh, I'm sorry, "Bang goes Byng".

2.   Quite frequently Sir Edwin had the habit of forgetting
Assistant's names, and invariably addressed them by some other
name not their own; One Assistant who rather resented being
continually addressed by Sir Edwin as Anderson for Adams,
thought he might attempt the same technique in return, and on
being greeted by Sir Edwin with the usual "Good morning Anderson", Adams retorted, "Good morning Sir Aston".

     ----

3.   A Yorkshire Industrialist for whom Sir Edwin designed
one of his best Country Houses, was rather apt at times to drop
a few 'h's. A visitor going over the House with Sir Edwin

when it was completed noted that a number of carved Keysones
had "H" incorporated in them, being the first letter of the
Client's name.

On inquiring their significance, Sir Edwin replied
that they were just of the few of the 'h's Mr Hemmingway had
dropped in the village.

[signature]

PAUL PHIPPS, F.R.I.B.A. *Chartered and Registered Architect*

TELEPHONE :
SLOANE 8186-7

14 PONT STREET
BELGRAVE SQUARE SW1

March 31st. 1939.

Dear Lutyens,

Since I got your letter I have been wondering
whether I could think of"any particularly pleasent or
amusing incident", which occurred during my time in
Sir Edwin's Office.   It's not likely that I can add
anything of much value to what you have already, but
here are a few notes of my time in 29, Bloomsbury
Square.

I was an articled pupil, and was there from 1901
to 1904.   There were always six or seven of us
draughtsmen, working in what was originally the Dining
Room, a fine room with panelling excellent to draw on
in charcoal at tea-time. Maxwell Ayrton, Horace
Farquharson, J. Lee, Norman Evill, O.P. Milne, John
Coleridge, Sid Evans, R. Huddart, "Beau" Hannen were all
there with me, and an excitable little American by name
Wallick, "of Indianapolis, Indiana, near Ohio".   Old
Barlow, Lutyens' first assistant, a tragic figure with a
tragic history, still sat bearded and silent under a

window, usually working out calculations with a slide-rule.

We knew, even in those days, that we were in the office of a great architect, and a very happy office it was. As I look back now, these are the sort of things I remember: the hours of serious work, and the moments of less serious play, with at times a good deal of rapid movement round the full-size board, (I think Lutlut must have been on a job then, or fishing, or both); the children looking in of an afternoon at tea-time on their way upstairs; a large doll's house that I seem to remember standing for a long time somewhere,in the Front Hall, I think (perhaps that was where the first idea of the Queen's Doll's House came from); Lutlut,never at a loss for any-thing except a light for his pipe, vainly picking at match-boxes pinned to the board beside the drawing he was correcting - "That's a hint, I suppose" -; being pushed off my bicycle by a bus-horse in Oxford Street (we came up to the Office a good deal on bicycles in those days); the dinner that Lutlut gave us at the Zoo and the visits behind the cages afterwards; ices at lunch time in the dim little refreshment room of the British Museum, etc., etc.

Then there were the Clients, or rather the legends about them, because, of course, they didn't

trouble us much.   There was the one who always referred
To Lutyens as "Kindly Light", because he led him on, and
the fat chef of another - this was before my time - so
circular on plan that he had to have a special circular
window in the Kitchen in case of fire, and the retired
Merchant who was said to want a room where he might rest
"half revealed and half concealed".   I measured his
house with the help of old Barlow, and that I think was
about the last job the old man ever did.   Sid Evans and
Hannen told me the other day that I killed him and hid
the body in Hampstead, but I have no recollection of this.

It was all a grand experience, and I am grateful
for having had it.   Of all that I learnt in Lutyens'
Office I am only doubtful of one thing.   He once told me
that if your india-rubber falls on the floor and you don't
know where it is, you should at once throw something over
your shoulder, and then when you look for the one you
ALWAYS find the other lying beside it! Not ALWAYS!

Even if these few lines are of no use to you, it
has been great fun remembering 29, Bloomsbury Square and
the good times and good fellows connected with it, so I
am much obliged to you for having written to me about it.

Eadred Lityens, Esq.,   Yours sincerely,
     A.R.I.B.A.,
1, Poet Hill,
HERTFORD.

E.J.T. Lutyens, Esq., A.R.I.B.A.,
1, Port Hill,
Hertford.

ROWAND ANDERSON & PAUL AND PARTNERS.
(Incorporating KININMONTH & SPENCE.)
ARCHITECTS.

W. HARDIE KININMONTH, A.R.I.B.A.
BASIL SPENCE, A.R.I.B.A.

TELEPHONE No. 20356.

16 RUTLAND SQUARE
EDINBURGH, 1.

24th. March, 1939.

Dear Mr. Lutyens,

I have just received your letter in which you refer to the possibility
of recording in some permanent form any amusing incidents that may have
happened during my period of employment in Sir Edwin's office.

I have told a great many of my friends of my interview before I was
accepted as a Junior Draughtsman.   I should explain that I came down to
London with the idea of seeking my fortune and I was determined to find
a job in one of the best offices in London.   An interview was granted
and my drawings were examined, I was then called into see Sir Edwin
himself and being very young and shy I was afraid, he looked at me over
his spectacles and announced that he was going to ask me a few questions
but the only question he asked me was whether I knew his portrait of an
"Indian Lady", then he sketched and demonstrated with lightning rapidity.
I think I must have been too surprised to even laugh but he patted me on
the back and said "its all right my boy you get the job".

Yours very truly,

Basil Spence.

30th March '39.

Dear Sir

Thank you for your letter.   I am interested
and glad to hear of your proposed ~~and~~ venture
and wish it every success.

I shall not forget my very first meeting
with Sir Edwin.   I had called to see if he
would employ me as an assistant and
was duly armed with some examples of my work.
He showed great interest in ~~these~~ my immature
drawings.   I had expected he would ask
me some tricky question on ~~prof~~ perhaps
building construction — but no.   He
gave me a slap on the backside! said, "I
like your face"!   I was to work for him.

Long live Sir Edwin!

Kenneth Thoms —

THOMAS WORTHINGTON
AND SONS, ARCHITECTS
Sir Percy S. Worthington,
M.A., Litt.D., F.S.A., F.R.I.B.A.
J. Hubert Worthington,
O.B.E., M.A., F.R.I.B.A.
T. Shirley S. Worthington,
A.R.I.B.A.

178, Oxford Road,
Manchester, 13.
Tel.: Ardwick 2745
2746

4 · 15 · 39

Dear Lutyens.

It was very disappointing to me that I could not
get up for the Old Lut Dinner to 'naughty lad'
but what a grand idea this is that anecdotes
should be collected in permanent form.

No doubt there will be a lot of overlapping, but I
enclose some rough jottings in case they may
be of use.

Yours very sincerely.

Hubert Worthington.

Lutyens Stories.

1912 - I had been working late at the office, so had
QAG.   the old man - I was leaving Queen Annes gate
        & he gave me a lift in his taxi.
        I said to him
        "Is it true, Sir, that you have a drawing
        board rigged up over your bath"
        Oh - does rumour say that - not exactly,
        but I use the children's slates".

        ———

        Lady Clients -
She   "And now, Mr Lutyens, in my new house
        tell me what shape will the nursery be"
He -   "Round of course, & then you've got no
        corners to put the kids in"

When he was selected as the architect for new
Delhi, Detmar Blow had been strongly backed
as runner up -
    He dashed into the office & said
            "Lutts for Delhi"
            "Won't Blow Blow"

A letter home from his first visit to Delhi said -
        "Delhi's a very hot place"
        "I call it OOZIPOOR"
"An elephant is a lovely animal for an Architect
to visit a job on, because you can pin down
your drawings any where you like on its back,
& you've only got to whistle & the trunk comes
up with the ___ ___"

Can't vouch for this – but.

Bishop. "Oh Sir Edwin, what a pity that you had no Christian Emblem on the Cenotaph"

Him. "To tell you the honest truth, my Lord, I was trying to design one article, uN 39."

Try & get him to tell the Story of Queen Mary & the drawing of the King bed in the Doll's House.
"This is the king, lying in bed – I hope you won't think it Lazy Majesty"
Queen M. "Lèse Majesté Sir Edwin"
He. "no. Lazy majesty – He's in bed."

Who's Who & Transcriptions

Whilst many young men passed through the office of Sir Edwin Lutyens, there is only room for brief biographies of those whose letters are reproduced here:

E.H. Beale, A.R.I.B.A.
Registered and Chartered Architect
Tel. Burwash 81.
Rockhurst,
Burwash,
Sussex.
7. 4. 39.

Dear Mr. Lutyens,

I think it an excellent idea to collect "Lut" stories in some permanent form, and I hope we shall all be able to acquire a copy of whatever you may produce.

The only personal thing I remember was when I took a staircase drawing to ask what was wanted. The stairs went up three sides of the well and the fourth side had a landing. Lutyens wanted the underside of the landing domed in its length and in its width. Both curves to be continued down on the soffit of the string of the stairs. He explained all this in his usual quick and inaudible way and ended by saying "You see, just cut it out of an orange". I did not see but was too alarmed to say so, being told "to take it away". And had to go and get help in the office.

A short while ago I met an artist at some friends here who had done some painting in Campion Hall Oxford for Lutyens. And he told me of his difficulties when trying to get sizes etc from Lut. How Lut mumbled and walked away from him round the table he following. And when it came to the dome, he too was told to "cut it out of an orange".

There was an elderly lady living here who in her youth remembered how shocked the Victorians were at a dance, when Lutyens' partner asked him if he did not think a certain girl very pretty and Lut said he did not, he was thinking what she would look like with no clothes on. But most of the best stories one only knows second hand. But I hope to find them all incorporated in your book.

Yours sincerely,
E.H. Beale

Carter, George Bertram (1896-1986)
EL assistant 1919-1922. Proponent of
the Streamline Moderne Style.

Bertram Carter. A.R.I.B.A .
28 Theobald's Road.
Grays Inn. London, W.C.I
Registered Chartered Architect
Telephone: Chancery 7980—Eltham
1673
April, Twenty One, 1939.

Eadred Lutyens, Esq., A.R.I.B.A.,
1 Port Hill, Hertford.

My dear Lutyens,
 I am quite ashamed of myself for my
neglect to your two letters and particularly tor missing the dinner to Sir
Edwin which I was very sorry not to
have attended.
 The one or two anecdotes which
I treasure I doubt if they are quite
suitable although charming in themselves. One in particular concerned
a glass soil pipe passing through
the drawing room at the Grange,
Rottingdean, and I would like to tell
you it. I expect you remember the
American Architect who visited us
and who had an introduction to Sir
Edwin. When this visitor related to
him that "We use your windows, your
doors, your dormers, your chimney
stacks in America", Sir Edwin replied:
"You go back and tell them to think
for themselves". Another one which
possibly Thomas has told you was a

little trouble over the datum pane.
Apparently some dormers looked into
a valley and it was structurally difficult
to work in the pane. Thomas after
a long argument complained that in
any case no one could see it to which
Sir Edwin snapped up: "yes they can".
"Well who can"? "Why, God can of
course". But these are not so nice as my
soil pipe which I simply must tell you.
 Kindest regards,
 Yours sincerely,
 Bertram Carter

Gardner, A. H.
Author of *Outline of English Architecture*,
1949.

C.M.C. Armstrong, F.R.I.B.A.
A. H. Gardiner, A.R.I.B.A.
Telephone 4755
19 Eaton Road,
Coventry
and at 39 High St., Warwick
25.3. 39.

Dear Mr. Lutyens,
 Thank you for your note. I should
hesitate to repeat the traditional office
stories as it is difficult to separate truth
from legend, though I should hate to
think that they belong to anything but
the first category.
 The enclosed office alphabet which
I was rash enough to compose may
however be of some interest. If you feel
a glossary is necessary, no doubt you
will let me know.

I have just been reminded of a ritual in the top office of Queen Anne's Gate. This consisted of lying on the central table (cleared for purpose) and climbing underneath and up the other side without touching the floor. I think most of us passed this test at one time or another. I also remember a hopping race on office stools (which I believe I won). This nearly brought the office down, in a literal manner.

Yours faithfully,
A.H. Gardiner.

E.J.T. Lutyens Esq., A.R.I.B.A.
1, Port Hill,
Hertford.

24.3.39.

AN OFFICE ALPHABET
for Sir Edwin Lutyens Office.

A stands for A.J.T. thankless his lot is,
B's the word blank, overworked by the office.
C's C.T. Ayerst whom we couldn't get first,
D are the drawings we've so often cursed,
E is Sir Edwin, our Master and Lord,
F are the Flappers we wave to when bored,
G's Garrett, Gardner and Greenwood as well,
H stands for Hough, our Liverpudlian swell.

I is the ink from India far,
J is for James who calls round with the car,
K is young Kain—that cheery young cod,
L is the angle of fifty four odd.
M is Macdonald our Badminton fan,
N's number 17, Home of the Clan,
O is for Owen, who thinks he can sing,
P stands for Percy—the abdomen king.
Q's Queen Anne's Gate, frequented by kites
R-rubber necking to see al the sights,
S is for Stewart, our oldest survivor,
T's office Tea—a much needed reviver.
U is the unit that E.L.L. favours,
V's Vincent Brooks whom we keep by our labours.
W's Miss Webb, our guardian and sister, and
X the excitement there'd be if we missed her.
Y's the young Butes we occasionally see, while
Z's quite impossible, as you'll agree.

A.H. Gardiner,
Jan. 1929.

Huddart, Richard Melville Fane

(AKA 'the Infant Prodigy') fl 1910-
14. Articled to ELL (1900-02) and
remained as improver (1903) and assistant (1904-5), travelled in France and
Italy; ARIBA 11/1907, proposers ELL,
S.T. Kitson, E.T. Hall. Commenced
practice1905 (Vol I pp 967-8).

4, Grosvenor Hill,
Wimbledon,
S.W. 19.
28.3.39.

Dear Mr Lutyens,

Owing to the war & being [illeg]
rather a dull dog anyhow, my memory
of incidents in Sir Edwin's office I not
too good.

I do however recollect that he made
in the kitchen of Lord Overstrand's
house an enormous circular window
the raison d'etre of which was not
quite obvious.

Sir Edwin explained that Lord
Overstrands' French chef being as
much a sphere as any human being
could be, the window was designed for
him to escape by in case of fire. What
could be more appropriate & fitting!

It was with great regret that I saw
someone else was made pope instead
of Sir Edwin as I had been hoping for
"another jolly dinner".

Yours sincerely
R.M.F. Huddart

Milne, Oswald Partridge
(1881-1968)

Born Enfield, Middlesex; son of an
architect; trained with Blomfield;
ELL assistant 1902; 1904 set up
his own practice with Paul Phipps;
projects mostly country houses but
also Claridges's Hotel and many school
buildings.

Oswald P. Milne F.R.I.B.A.
Architect.
Chartered & Registered
Welbeck 7105
64 Wigmore Street,
London, W.1.
3rd May 1939.

Dear Eadrid,

I received your printed form asking
for incidents that happened when one
was in Sir Edwin's Office.

I have nothing very definite to relate,
but I have put down a few notes of
abiding impressions of that time.

Alas! you should have said over a
period of 40 years and not 30, that Sir
Edwin had congenial relations with
his assistants and pupils. It was in the
very early years of the century that I
spent some two years in the office in
Bloomsbury Square.

We were then all youthful assistants
of a young master who was already
earning famewith his imaginative
and charming country houses and
his inventive use of materials. His
reputation was already becoming

international as was shown by the fact that Wallick, an American, and Bamford, a New Zealander, on their arrival in England had insisted on becoming his pupils.

Assistants and pupils all worked together in the large room behind E.L.L.'s front room office. 'Syd' Evans, who must be known to many who have passed through the office, was already well established in the office traditions when I arrived as an assistant. He had his own peculiar dry jokes and stories. One of the most honoured of these was of the waiter who walked so much in serving his clients that he wore off his feet and then had to turn up the ends of his legs so as to carry on.

Paul Phipps, just down from Oxford, had a ready pencil as a caricaturist, and combining this with wit, banter and leg pull, he would drive Wallick to fury, after which he would insist on shaking hands with "hands across the sea, Wallick, hands across the sea".

There were as pupils, Huddart, from a Yorkshire Rectory, better known as the 'Infant Prodigy' and Beau Hannen, who from the building tradition of his family, was destined by them to be an Architect, but whose heart was more upon stage matters than on half inch and full size details. Presently he abandoned the 'noble art' and became famous as Nicholas Hannen, the actor.

In those days E.L.L. lived above the shop and there was a certain domestic air about the offices on the ground floor. The young family, consisting at that time of 'Barbie' and Robert, were often, on returning from their afternoon walk, brought into the office by their nurse, and were regaled with lumps of sugar. Tea was sure to be brewing, for Alwyn, who had joined the Staff, used to start boiling the kettle as soon as he returned from lunch.

Lutyens himself was a great worker, and very often descended to the office again after dinner and worked till midnight, and for weeks together, if there was a press of work, we would return to our drawing boards after a dinner interval and continue translating the sketches that flowed from our Master's pencil into working drawings.
Yours sincerely,
Oswald P. Milne

Owen, Trevor
One of 'the Stayers'; ELL assistant 1925-1935.

Trevor Owen, A.R.I.B.A.,
Chartered Architect.
Tel: PAD. 6841
118, George Street,
London, W.1.
March 29th. 1939

Dear Mr Lutyens,
In reply to your request for anecdotes relating to Sir Edwin, I recall the following amusing stories if you think

them worth recording in your permanent collection.

During a visit to a London House to which Sir Edwin was making additions and alterations, a newsboy passed by with a placard headline in large type, "Lord Byng dead". The Client who happened to be a retired Army Colonel remarked to Sir Edwin, "By jove, Byng's dead", and Sir Edwin's immediate reply was, Oh, I'm sorry, "Bang goes Byng".

Quite frequently Sir Edwin had the habit of forgetting Assistant's names, and invariably addressed them by some other name not their own; One Assistant who rather resented being continually addressed by Sir Edwin as Anderson for Adams, thought he might attempt the same technique in return, and on being greeted by Sir Edwin with the usual "Good morning Anderson", Adams retorted, "Good morning Sir Aston".

A Yorkshire Industrialist for whom Sir Edwin designed one of his best Country Houses, was rather apt at times to drop a few 'h's. A visitor going over the House with Sir Edwin when it was completed noted that a number of carved Keysones [sic] had "H" incorporated in them, being the first letter of the Client's name. On inquiring their significance, Sir Edwin replied that they were just a few of the 'h's Mr Hemingway had dropped in the village.
Trevor Owen.

Phipps, the Hon Paul (1880—1953)
Born New York; ELL assistant 1901-1904; established his own practice in London; in Vancouver, Canada by 1911-1914 in partnership with Hoult Horton (Horton & Phipps); 1919 in practice with Oswald Milne (Phipps & Milne); projects mostly country houses but includes the Christian Scientist's church in Kensington; author of many amusing sketches/cartoons now in the RIBA Collection; his daughter was the actress Joyce Grenfell.

PAUL PHIPPS, F.R.I.B.A. Chartered and Registered Architect
TELEPHONE :
SLOANE 8186-7
14 PONT STREET
BELGRAVE SQUARE SW I
March 31st. 1939.

Dear Lutyens,

Since I got your letter I have been wondering whether I could think of "any particularly pleasant or amusing incident", which occurred during my time in Sir Edwin' s Office. It's not likely that I can add anything of much value to what you have already, but here are a few notes of my time in 29, Bloomsbury Square.

I was an articled pupil, and was there from 1901 to 1904. There were always six or seven of us draughtsmen, working in what was originally the Dining Room, a fine room with panelling excellent to draw on in charcoal at tea-time.

Maxwell Ayrton, Horace Farquharson, J. Lee, Norman Evill, O.P. Milne, John Coleridge, Sid Evans, R. Huddart, "Beau" Hannen were all there with me, and an excitable little American by name Wallick, "of Indianapolis, Indiana, near Ohio". Old Barlow, Lutyens' first assistant, a tragic figure with a tragic history, still sat bearded and silent under a window, usually working out calculations with a slide rule.

We knew, even in those days, that we were in the office of a great architect, and a very happy office it was. As I look back now, these are the sort of things I remember: the hours of serious work, and the moments of less serious play, with at times a good deal of rapid movement round the full-size board, (I think Lutlut must have been on a job then, or fishing, or both); the children looking in of an afternoon at tea-time on their way upstairs; a large doll's house that I seem to remember standing for a long time somewhere, in the Front Hall, I think (perhaps that was where the first idea of the Queen's Doll's House cane from); Lutlut, never at a loss for anything except a light for his pipe, vainly picking at match-boxes pinned to the board beside the drawing he was correcting—"That's a hint, I suppose"—; being pushed off my bicycle by a bus-horse in Oxford Street (we came up to the Office a good deal on bicycles in those days); the dinner that Lutlut gave us at the Zoo and the visits behind the cages afterwards; ices at lunch time in

Lut sketched by Charles Mahoney

the dim little refreshment room of the British Museum, etc., etc.

Then there were the Clients, or rather the legends about them, because, of course, they didn't trouble us much. There was the one who always referred to Lutyens as "Kindly Light", because he led him on, and the fat chef of another—this was before my time—so circular on plan that he had to have a special circular window in the Kitchen in case of fire, and the retired Merchant who was said to want a room where he might rest "half revealed and half concealed". I measured his house with the help of old Barlow, and that I think was about the last job the old man ever did. Sid Evans and Hannen told me the other day that I killed him and hid the body in Hampstead, but I have no recollection of this.

It was all a grand experience, and I am grateful for having had it. Of all that I learnt in Lutyens' Office I am only doubtful of one thing. He once told me that if your india-rubber falls on the floor and you don't know where it is, you should at once throw, something over your shoulder, and then when you look for the one you ALWAYS find the other lying beside it! Not ALWAYS!

Even if these few lines are of no use to you, it has been great fun remembering 29, Bloomsbury Square and the good times and good fellows connected with it, so I am much obliged to you for having written to me about it.

Yours sincerely,
Paul Phipps

Eadred Lutyens, Esq.,
A.R.I.B.A.,
1, Poet Hill,
HERTFORD.

Spence, Sir Basil Urwin (1907-1976)

Born India but essentially Scottish; ELL assistant 1929-1930; a Modernist/ Brutalist architect whose works include: Coventry Cathedral, Hyde Park barracks and the New Zealand parliament building in Wellington.

E.J.T. Lutyens, Esq., A.R.I.B.A.,
1, Port Hill,
Hertford.
Rowand Anderson & Paul and Partners.
(Incorporating Kininmonth & Spence.)
Architects.
W. Hardie Kininmonth, A.R.I.B.A.
Basil Spence, A.R.I.B.A.
Telephone No. 20356
16 Rutland Square
Edinburgh, 1.
24th. March, 1939.

Dear Mr. Lutyens,

I have just received your letter in which you refer to the possibility of recording in some permanent form any amusing incidents that may have happened during my period of employment in Sir Edwin's office.

I have told a great many of my friends of my interview before I was accepted as a Junior Draughtsman. I should explain that I came down to London with the idea of seeking my fortune and I was determined to find a job in one of the best offices in London. An interview was granted and my drawings were examined, I was then called into see Sir Edwin himself and being very young and shy I was afraid, he looked at me over his spectacles and announced that he was going to ask me a few questions but the only question he asked me was whether I knew his portrait of an "Indian Lady", this he sketched and demonstrated with lightning rapidity. I think I must have been too surprised to even laugh but he patted me on the back and said, "its all right my boy you get the job".

Yours very truly,
Basil Spence.

Thoms, Kenneth Ogilvie (1915-1984)

Born Edinburgh; ELL assistant 1937.

14 Coates Gardens,
Edinburgh, 12.
30th March '39.

Dear Sir

Thank you for your letter. I am interested and glad to hear of your proposed venture and wish it every success.

I shall not forget my very first meeting with Sir Edwin. I had called to see if he would employ me as an assistant and was duly armed with some examples of my work. He showed great interest in my immature drawings. I had expected he would ask me some tricky question on perhaps building construction—but no. He gave me a slap on the backside! Said, "I like your face"! I was to work for him.

Long live Sir Edwin!
Kenneth Thoms

Worthington, Sir John Hubert (1886-1963)

Born Stockport; son of an architect; ELL assistant 1912-1914; after the war rejoined the family firm in Manchester; 1923 professor at the Royal College of Art, London; returned to Thomas Worthington & Son; projects include university buildings in oxford, numerous war memorials and restoration after WW2.

Thomas Worthington and Sons,
Architects
Sir Percy S. Worthington, M.A., Litt D., F.R.I.B.A.
J. Hubert Worthington, O.B.E., M.A., F.R.I.B.A.
T. Shirley S. Worthington, A.R.I.B.A.
178, Oxford Road,
Manchester, 13.
Tel.: Ardwick 2745 2746
4.IV.39

Dear Lutyens,

It was very disappointing to me that I could not get up for the Old Lut Dinner to 'Naughty Ned' but what a grand idea this is that anecdotes should be collected in permanent form.

No doubt there will be a lot of overlapping, but I enclose some rough jottings in case they may be of use.
Your very sincere,
Hubert Worthington.

Lutyens Stories

1912 QAG—I had been working late at the office, so had the old man—I was leaving Queen Annes Gate & he gave me a lift in his taxi.
I said to him
"Is it true, sir, that you have a drawing board rigged up over your bath"
"Oh—does rumour say that—not exactly, but I use the children's slates".

Lady Client —
She "And now, Mr Lutyens, in my new house tell me what shape will the nursery be?"
He—"Round of course, & then you've got no corners to put the kids in".

When he was selected as the architect for New Delhi, Detmar Blow had been strongly backed as runner up —
He dashed into the office & said
"I've got Delhi"
"Won't Blow Blow"

A letter home from his first visit to Delhi said —
"Delhi's a very hot place
I call it Oozipoor."
"An elephant is a lovely animal for an Architect to visit a job on, because you can pin down your drawings anywhere you like on its back, & you've only got to whistle & the trunk comes up with the India rubber."

Cant vouch for this—but—

Bishop: "Oh Sir Edwin, what a pity that you had no Christian emblem on the Cenotaph".
Him: "To tell you the honest truth, my Lord, I was trying to design one article, not 39".

Try & get him to tell the story of Queen Mary & the drawings of the King's bed in the Doll's House.
["]This is the King, lying in bed—I hope you won't think it Lazy Majesty["].
Queen M—"Lèse Majesté Sir Edwin".
He—"No—Lazy Majesty—He's in bed".

Unknown

3 London Road,
High Wycombe.
Bucks.
March 28th. 1939.

Eadrid Lutyens, Esq.
1 Port Hill,
Hertford.

Dear Sir.
    In reply to your letter re. the collection of anecdotes concerning Sir Edwin, I add a few below which I hope may be of some use to you.
    I am afraid that, compared with most of the tales about Sir Edwin, these

are very trivial, but I have restricted my efforts to incidents in which I was more or less involved or for which I can personally vouch.

The first occurred after I had been with him for a mere six months. By means of living on bread and water for that period I had scraped together enough hard cash to buy a copy of "Houses and Gardens".

One day, greatly daring, I took it down to him for him to sign. He was very charming about it all and sat down, pen in hand, mumbling vaguely "Dearmewashallput?" (I am afraid it is quite impossible to convey on this type-writer those quaint, sort of ade-noidal, sounds that he produces when he is talking of one thing and thinking of something entirely different!) After a moment he wrote, to my amazement and my surprise—"In great regard", E.L.L. I was just thinking what the devil of a fellow I must be to receive such an inscription after a mere six months when Sir Edwin turned round and said, "I have put "In great regard", as I thought there might be a blank cheque under the page! Still, when I shew the book to my friends they naturally think what I first thought and I hate disillusioning them, so it works out alright in the long run!

One afternoon a friend of mine was rushing downstairs with an eaves detail for which the printer was waiting. As he was passing Sir Edwin's room, Sir Edwin came wandering out and demanded to know what he (Bailey) had got. Bailey, in a great hurry just said "Eaves Sir,—full size detail". "Oh" replied Sir Edwin, "Haven't you done a full size of Adam's as well!"

Mr. Stewart will no doubt vouch for some of the next as he was directly con-cerned. He had just done some drawings for a War Memorial in Rhodesia and the job had been estimated at a simply prohibitive figure. As the drawing stood there were no dimensions on it, merely the scale. With great resource Sir Edwin remarked "Oh, never mind, alter the scale from ¼" to ½" and see what it comes out at!" This actually gave a figure of less than a quarter the original one, and I believe that it was submitted to the authorities in this form!

I am afraid that I cannot remember any more, that I have any right to relate, but will let you have any that may occur to me within the next week or so.

If there is any publication resultant from these united efforts I shall be most grateful to be allowed to sub-scribe, within the normally restricted limits of a younger member of this impecunious profession! With many thanks and all best wishes in your search,

Yours faithfully,
[Signature lost]

Acknowledgments

FIRST, I would like to thank Dr Mervyn Miller, Architect, Town Planner and trustee of the Lutyens Trust, for his encouragement and advice when I began to plan this. Next, Margaret Richardson OBE, a great expert on Lutyens, one of the principal organisers of the landmark 1981 Lutyens Exhibition at the Hayward Gallery which effectively rekindled the reputation of Sir Edwin Lutyens—she may not know it but the exhibition catalogue to which she was the chief contributor has been invaluable—thank you! My thanks to those who have contributed some of the images, Candia Lutyens, Charles Hind, Chief Curator RIBA Drawings Collection, and The Master of Campion Hall, Oxford. And my thanks to those who have helped (or have offered to help) Martin Lutyens, Charles Lutyens, Clive Aslet, current Chairman of the Lutyens Trust, Sarah Lutyens, Catriona Turvill (née Lutyens), Robin Prater, Executive Director of the Lutyens Trust America, and Anthony Eyre at the Mount Orleans Press for his patience and good advice.

Illustrations

Drawn by Sir E Lutyens
Savinirne club dinner Mar 18
1930

what a honour